DEDICATION

This Mileage Log Book is dedicated to all the people out there who need to record their mileage for either work or personal and document their findings in the process.

You are my inspiration for producing books and I'm honored to be a part of keeping all of your Mileage notes, and records organized.

This journal notebook will help you record your details about your vehicle's mileage.

Thoughtfully put together with these sections to record: Date, Vehicle Information, Destination, Purpose, Odometer Start & End, & Total Mileage.

HOW TO USE THIS BOOK

The purpose of this book is to keep all of your Mileage notes all in one place. It will help keep you organized.

This MIleage Log Book will allow you to accurately document every detail about your mileage. It's a great way to chart your course by recording your mileage accurately.

Here are examples of the prompts for you to fill in and write about your experience in this book:

1. Date - Write the date of the odometer reading.
2. Make, Model & Year - Log your vehicle's Make, Model, & Year.
3. Odometer Start - Record the odometer reading at the start of the trip.
4. Odometer End - Write the odometer reading at the end of the trip.
5. Destination/ Purpose - Log the purpose of your trip and where you are going.
6. Total - Record the total number of miles for the entire trip.

MILEAGE LOG

MAKE:		MODEL:		YEAR:
DATE:	ODOMETER: START | END		TOTAL:	DESTINATION / PURPOSE:

MILEAGE LOG

MAKE:		MODEL:		YEAR:
DATE:	ODOMETER: START | END		TOTAL:	DESTINATION / PURPOSE:

MILEAGE LOG

MAKE:		MODEL:		YEAR:
DATE:	**ODOMETER: START | END**		**TOTAL:**	**DESTINATION / PURPOSE:**

MILEAGE LOG

MAKE:		MODEL:		YEAR:
DATE:	ODOMETER: START | END		TOTAL:	DESTINATION / PURPOSE:

MILEAGE LOG

MAKE:		MODEL:		YEAR:
DATE:	ODOMETER: START | END		TOTAL:	DESTINATION / PURPOSE:

MILEAGE LOG

MAKE:		MODEL:		YEAR:
DATE:	ODOMETER: START | END		TOTAL:	DESTINATION / PURPOSE:

MILEAGE LOG

MAKE:		MODEL:		YEAR:
DATE:	ODOMETER: START | END		TOTAL:	DESTINATION / PURPOSE:

MILEAGE LOG

MAKE:		MODEL:		YEAR:
DATE:	ODOMETER: START | END		TOTAL:	DESTINATION / PURPOSE:

MILEAGE LOG

MAKE:		MODEL:		YEAR:
DATE:	**ODOMETER: START | END**		**TOTAL:**	**DESTINATION / PURPOSE:**

MILEAGE LOG

MAKE:		MODEL:		YEAR:
DATE:	ODOMETER: START | END		TOTAL:	DESTINATION / PURPOSE:

MILEAGE LOG

MAKE:		MODEL:		YEAR:
DATE:	**ODOMETER: START | END**		**TOTAL:**	**DESTINATION / PURPOSE:**

MILEAGE LOG

MAKE:		MODEL:		YEAR:
DATE:	ODOMETER: START | END		TOTAL:	DESTINATION / PURPOSE:

MILEAGE LOG

MAKE:		MODEL:		YEAR:
DATE:	**ODOMETER: START | END**		**TOTAL:**	**DESTINATION / PURPOSE:**

MILEAGE LOG

MAKE:		MODEL:		YEAR:
DATE:	ODOMETER: START	END	TOTAL:	DESTINATION / PURPOSE:

MILEAGE LOG

MAKE:		MODEL:		YEAR:
DATE:	ODOMETER: START | END		TOTAL:	DESTINATION / PURPOSE:

MILEAGE LOG

MAKE:		MODEL:		YEAR:
DATE:	ODOMETER: START | END		TOTAL:	DESTINATION / PURPOSE:

MILEAGE LOG

MAKE:		MODEL:		YEAR:
DATE:	ODOMETER: START | END		TOTAL:	DESTINATION / PURPOSE:

MILEAGE LOG

MAKE:		MODEL:		YEAR:
DATE:	ODOMETER: START | END		TOTAL:	DESTINATION / PURPOSE:

MILEAGE LOG

MAKE:		MODEL:		YEAR:
DATE:	**ODOMETER: START | END**		**TOTAL:**	**DESTINATION / PURPOSE:**

MILEAGE LOG

MAKE:		MODEL:		YEAR:
DATE:	ODOMETER: START | END		TOTAL:	DESTINATION / PURPOSE:

MILEAGE LOG

MAKE:		MODEL:		YEAR:
DATE:	ODOMETER: START | END		TOTAL:	DESTINATION / PURPOSE:

MILEAGE LOG

MAKE:		MODEL:		YEAR:
DATE:	ODOMETER: START | END		TOTAL:	DESTINATION / PURPOSE:

MILEAGE LOG

<table>
<tr><td colspan="2">MAKE:</td><td colspan="2">MODEL:</td><td>YEAR:</td></tr>
<tr><td>DATE:</td><td colspan="2">ODOMETER:
START | END</td><td>TOTAL:</td><td>DESTINATION / PURPOSE:</td></tr>
<tr><td></td><td></td><td></td><td></td><td></td></tr>
<tr><td></td><td></td><td></td><td></td><td></td></tr>
<tr><td></td><td></td><td></td><td></td><td></td></tr>
<tr><td></td><td></td><td></td><td></td><td></td></tr>
<tr><td></td><td></td><td></td><td></td><td></td></tr>
<tr><td></td><td></td><td></td><td></td><td></td></tr>
<tr><td></td><td></td><td></td><td></td><td></td></tr>
<tr><td></td><td></td><td></td><td></td><td></td></tr>
<tr><td></td><td></td><td></td><td></td><td></td></tr>
<tr><td></td><td></td><td></td><td></td><td></td></tr>
<tr><td></td><td></td><td></td><td></td><td></td></tr>
<tr><td></td><td></td><td></td><td></td><td></td></tr>
<tr><td></td><td></td><td></td><td></td><td></td></tr>
<tr><td></td><td></td><td></td><td></td><td></td></tr>
<tr><td></td><td></td><td></td><td></td><td></td></tr>
</table>

MILEAGE LOG

MAKE:		MODEL:		YEAR:
DATE:	ODOMETER: START | END		TOTAL:	DESTINATION / PURPOSE:

MILEAGE LOG

MAKE:		MODEL:		YEAR:
DATE:	**ODOMETER: START | END**		**TOTAL:**	**DESTINATION / PURPOSE:**

MILEAGE LOG

MAKE:		MODEL:		YEAR:
DATE:	ODOMETER: START | END		TOTAL:	DESTINATION / PURPOSE:

MILEAGE LOG

MAKE:		MODEL:		YEAR:
DATE:	ODOMETER: START | END		TOTAL:	DESTINATION / PURPOSE:

MILEAGE LOG

MAKE:		MODEL:		YEAR:
DATE:	ODOMETER: START | END		TOTAL:	DESTINATION / PURPOSE:

MILEAGE LOG

MAKE:		MODEL:		YEAR:
DATE:	ODOMETER: START | END		TOTAL:	DESTINATION / PURPOSE:

MILEAGE LOG

MAKE:		MODEL:		YEAR:
DATE:	ODOMETER: START | END		TOTAL:	DESTINATION / PURPOSE:

MILEAGE LOG

MAKE:		MODEL:		YEAR:
DATE:	ODOMETER: START | END		TOTAL:	DESTINATION / PURPOSE:

MILEAGE LOG

MAKE:		MODEL:		YEAR:
DATE:	ODOMETER: START | END		TOTAL:	DESTINATION / PURPOSE:

MILEAGE LOG

MAKE:		MODEL:		YEAR:
DATE:	ODOMETER: START | END		TOTAL:	DESTINATION / PURPOSE:

MILEAGE LOG

MAKE:		MODEL:		YEAR:
DATE:	ODOMETER: START | END		TOTAL:	DESTINATION / PURPOSE:

MILEAGE LOG

MAKE:		MODEL:		YEAR:
DATE:	**ODOMETER: START | END**		**TOTAL:**	**DESTINATION / PURPOSE:**

MILEAGE LOG

MAKE:		MODEL:		YEAR:
DATE:	ODOMETER: START | END		TOTAL:	DESTINATION / PURPOSE:

MILEAGE LOG

MAKE:		MODEL:		YEAR:
DATE:	ODOMETER: START | END		TOTAL:	DESTINATION / PURPOSE:

MILEAGE LOG

MAKE:		MODEL:		YEAR:
DATE:	ODOMETER: START | END		TOTAL:	DESTINATION / PURPOSE:

MILEAGE LOG

MAKE:		MODEL:		YEAR:
DATE:	ODOMETER: START | END		TOTAL:	DESTINATION / PURPOSE:

MILEAGE LOG

MAKE:		MODEL:		YEAR:
DATE:	ODOMETER: START | END		TOTAL:	DESTINATION / PURPOSE:

MILEAGE LOG

MAKE:		MODEL:		YEAR:
DATE:	ODOMETER: START | END		TOTAL:	DESTINATION / PURPOSE:

MILEAGE LOG

MAKE:		MODEL:		YEAR:
DATE:	ODOMETER: START | END		TOTAL:	DESTINATION / PURPOSE:

MILEAGE LOG

MAKE:		MODEL:		YEAR:
DATE:	ODOMETER: START | END		TOTAL:	DESTINATION / PURPOSE:

MILEAGE LOG

MAKE:		MODEL:		YEAR:
DATE:	ODOMETER: START | END		TOTAL:	DESTINATION / PURPOSE:

MILEAGE LOG

MAKE:		MODEL:		YEAR:
DATE:	ODOMETER: START | END		TOTAL:	DESTINATION / PURPOSE:

MILEAGE LOG

MAKE:		MODEL:		YEAR:
DATE:	ODOMETER: START | END		TOTAL:	DESTINATION / PURPOSE:

MILEAGE LOG

MAKE:		MODEL:		YEAR:
DATE:	ODOMETER: START | END		TOTAL:	DESTINATION / PURPOSE:

MILEAGE LOG

MAKE:		MODEL:		YEAR:
DATE:	ODOMETER: START | END		TOTAL:	DESTINATION / PURPOSE:

MILEAGE LOG

MAKE:		MODEL:		YEAR:
DATE:	ODOMETER: START | END		TOTAL:	DESTINATION / PURPOSE:

MILEAGE LOG

MAKE:		MODEL:		YEAR:
DATE:	ODOMETER: START | END		TOTAL:	DESTINATION / PURPOSE:

MILEAGE LOG

MAKE:		MODEL:		YEAR:
DATE:	ODOMETER: START | END		TOTAL:	DESTINATION / PURPOSE:

MILEAGE LOG

MAKE:		MODEL:		YEAR:
DATE:	ODOMETER: START | END		TOTAL:	DESTINATION / PURPOSE:

MILEAGE LOG

MAKE:		MODEL:		YEAR:
DATE:	ODOMETER: START | END		TOTAL:	DESTINATION / PURPOSE:

MILEAGE LOG

MAKE:		MODEL:		YEAR:
DATE:	**ODOMETER: START | END**		**TOTAL:**	**DESTINATION / PURPOSE:**

MILEAGE LOG

MAKE:		MODEL:		YEAR:
DATE:	ODOMETER: START | END		TOTAL:	DESTINATION / PURPOSE:

MILEAGE LOG

MAKE:		MODEL:		YEAR:
DATE:	ODOMETER: START | END		TOTAL:	DESTINATION / PURPOSE:

MILEAGE LOG

MAKE:		MODEL:		YEAR:
DATE:	**ODOMETER: START | END**		**TOTAL:**	**DESTINATION / PURPOSE:**

MILEAGE LOG

MAKE:		MODEL:		YEAR:
DATE:	ODOMETER: START | END		TOTAL:	DESTINATION / PURPOSE:

MILEAGE LOG

MAKE:		MODEL:		YEAR:
DATE:	ODOMETER: START | END		TOTAL:	DESTINATION / PURPOSE:

MILEAGE LOG

MAKE:		MODEL:		YEAR:
DATE:	ODOMETER: START | END		TOTAL:	DESTINATION / PURPOSE:

MILEAGE LOG

MAKE:		MODEL:		YEAR:
DATE:	ODOMETER: START | END		TOTAL:	DESTINATION / PURPOSE:

MILEAGE LOG

MAKE:		MODEL:		YEAR:
DATE:	ODOMETER: START | END		TOTAL:	DESTINATION / PURPOSE:

MILEAGE LOG

MAKE:		MODEL:		YEAR:
DATE:	ODOMETER: START	END	TOTAL:	DESTINATION / PURPOSE:

MILEAGE LOG

MAKE:		MODEL:		YEAR:
DATE:	ODOMETER: START | END		TOTAL:	DESTINATION / PURPOSE:

MILEAGE LOG

MAKE:		MODEL:		YEAR:
DATE:	ODOMETER: START | END		TOTAL:	DESTINATION / PURPOSE:

MILEAGE LOG

MAKE:		MODEL:		YEAR:
DATE:	ODOMETER: START | END		TOTAL:	DESTINATION / PURPOSE:

MILEAGE LOG

MAKE:		MODEL:		YEAR:
DATE:	ODOMETER: START | END		TOTAL:	DESTINATION / PURPOSE:

MILEAGE LOG

MAKE:		MODEL:		YEAR:
DATE:	ODOMETER: START | END		TOTAL:	DESTINATION / PURPOSE:

MILEAGE LOG

MAKE:		MODEL:		YEAR:
DATE:	ODOMETER: START | END		TOTAL:	DESTINATION / PURPOSE:

MILEAGE LOG

MAKE:		MODEL:		YEAR:
DATE:	ODOMETER: START | END		TOTAL:	DESTINATION / PURPOSE:

MILEAGE LOG

MAKE:		MODEL:		YEAR:
DATE:	ODOMETER: START | END		TOTAL:	DESTINATION / PURPOSE:

MILEAGE LOG

MAKE:		MODEL:		YEAR:
DATE:	ODOMETER: START | END		TOTAL:	DESTINATION / PURPOSE:

MILEAGE LOG

MAKE:		MODEL:		YEAR:
DATE:	ODOMETER: START | END		TOTAL:	DESTINATION / PURPOSE:

MILEAGE LOG

MAKE:		MODEL:		YEAR:
DATE:	ODOMETER: START | END		TOTAL:	DESTINATION / PURPOSE:

MILEAGE LOG

MAKE:		MODEL:		YEAR:
DATE:	ODOMETER: START | END		TOTAL:	DESTINATION / PURPOSE:

MILEAGE LOG

MAKE:		**MODEL:**		**YEAR:**
DATE:	**ODOMETER: START | END**		**TOTAL:**	**DESTINATION / PURPOSE:**

MILEAGE LOG

MAKE:		MODEL:		YEAR:
DATE:	ODOMETER: START | END		TOTAL:	DESTINATION / PURPOSE:

MILEAGE LOG

MAKE:		MODEL:		YEAR:
DATE:	ODOMETER: START | END		TOTAL:	DESTINATION / PURPOSE:

MILEAGE LOG

MAKE:		MODEL:		YEAR:
DATE:	**ODOMETER: START | END**		**TOTAL:**	**DESTINATION / PURPOSE:**

MILEAGE LOG

MAKE:		MODEL:		YEAR:
DATE:	ODOMETER: START | END		TOTAL:	DESTINATION / PURPOSE:

MILEAGE LOG

MAKE:		MODEL:		YEAR:
DATE:	ODOMETER: START | END		TOTAL:	DESTINATION / PURPOSE:

MILEAGE LOG

MAKE:		MODEL:		YEAR:
DATE:	ODOMETER: START | END		TOTAL:	DESTINATION / PURPOSE:

MILEAGE LOG

MAKE:		MODEL:		YEAR:
DATE:	ODOMETER: START | END		TOTAL:	DESTINATION / PURPOSE:

MILEAGE LOG

MAKE:		MODEL:		YEAR:
DATE:	ODOMETER: START | END		TOTAL:	DESTINATION / PURPOSE:

MILEAGE LOG

<table>
<tr><td colspan="2">MAKE:</td><td colspan="2">MODEL:</td><td>YEAR:</td></tr>
<tr><td>DATE:</td><td colspan="2">ODOMETER:
START | END</td><td>TOTAL:</td><td>DESTINATION /
PURPOSE:</td></tr>
<tr><td></td><td></td><td></td><td></td><td></td></tr>
<tr><td></td><td></td><td></td><td></td><td></td></tr>
<tr><td></td><td></td><td></td><td></td><td></td></tr>
<tr><td></td><td></td><td></td><td></td><td></td></tr>
<tr><td></td><td></td><td></td><td></td><td></td></tr>
<tr><td></td><td></td><td></td><td></td><td></td></tr>
<tr><td></td><td></td><td></td><td></td><td></td></tr>
<tr><td></td><td></td><td></td><td></td><td></td></tr>
<tr><td></td><td></td><td></td><td></td><td></td></tr>
<tr><td></td><td></td><td></td><td></td><td></td></tr>
<tr><td></td><td></td><td></td><td></td><td></td></tr>
<tr><td></td><td></td><td></td><td></td><td></td></tr>
<tr><td></td><td></td><td></td><td></td><td></td></tr>
<tr><td></td><td></td><td></td><td></td><td></td></tr>
<tr><td></td><td></td><td></td><td></td><td></td></tr>
</table>

MILEAGE LOG

MAKE:		MODEL:		YEAR:
DATE:	**ODOMETER: START**	**END**	**TOTAL:**	**DESTINATION / PURPOSE:**

MILEAGE LOG

MAKE:		MODEL:		YEAR:
DATE:	ODOMETER: START | END		TOTAL:	DESTINATION / PURPOSE:

MILEAGE LOG

MAKE:		MODEL:		YEAR:
DATE:	ODOMETER: START | END		TOTAL:	DESTINATION / PURPOSE:

MILEAGE LOG

MAKE:		MODEL:		YEAR:
DATE:	ODOMETER: START | END		TOTAL:	DESTINATION / PURPOSE:

MILEAGE LOG

MAKE:		MODEL:		YEAR:
DATE:	ODOMETER: START | END		TOTAL:	DESTINATION / PURPOSE:

MILEAGE LOG

MAKE:		MODEL:		YEAR:
DATE:	**ODOMETER: START | END**		**TOTAL:**	**DESTINATION / PURPOSE:**

MILEAGE LOG

MAKE:		MODEL:		YEAR:
DATE:	ODOMETER: START | END		TOTAL:	DESTINATION / PURPOSE:

MILEAGE LOG

MAKE:		MODEL:		YEAR:
DATE:	ODOMETER: START | END		TOTAL:	DESTINATION / PURPOSE:

MILEAGE LOG

MAKE:		MODEL:		YEAR:
DATE:	ODOMETER: START | END		TOTAL:	DESTINATION / PURPOSE:

MILEAGE LOG

MAKE:		MODEL:		YEAR:
DATE:	**ODOMETER: START | END**		**TOTAL:**	**DESTINATION / PURPOSE:**

MILEAGE LOG

MAKE:		MODEL:		YEAR:
DATE:	ODOMETER: START | END		TOTAL:	DESTINATION / PURPOSE:

MILEAGE LOG

MAKE:		MODEL:		YEAR:
DATE:	ODOMETER: START | END		TOTAL:	DESTINATION / PURPOSE:

MILEAGE LOG

MAKE:		MODEL:		YEAR:
DATE:	ODOMETER: START | END		TOTAL:	DESTINATION / PURPOSE:

www.ingramcontent.com/pod-product-compliance
Lightning Source LLC
Chambersburg PA
CBHW071407080526
44587CB00017B/3206
* 9 7 8 1 6 4 9 4 4 2 6 7 3 *